ANOTHER TIME ANOTHER PLACE

TOWARDS AN AUSTRALIAN CHURCH

GLENN LOUGHREY

COVENTRY
PRESS

Published in Australia by
Coventry Press
33 Scoresby Road
Bayswater Vic. 3153
Australia

ISBN 9780648360186

Scripture quotations are from the *New Revised Standard Version Bible*, copyright 1989, Division of Christian Education of the National Council of the Churches of Christ in the United States of America. Used by permission. All rights reserved.

Cataloguing-in-Publication entry is available from the National Library of Australia http:/catalogue.nla.gov.au/.

Cover image 'Invasion' and chapter sketches by Glenn Loughrey

Text design by Film Shot Graphics
Cover design by Ian James - www.jgd.com.au

Printed in Australia

Contents

Preface:
Embracing Change
with Discernment

In every decision we make as persons, groups or nations we choose between continuing an established and comfortable pattern, or making some change great or small. Established routines provide stability and a degree of confidence that they are right. They attract explanatory frameworks to defend them against change. To the question, 'why do you that, or do it that way?' the often heard answer takes the forms of 'I always have', 'it's traditional', 'it's the way things are', 'It worked in the past'. Change involves risk, uncertainty, faith.

We are confronted with the need to change when what we have been doing cannot be said to be working. This is where the Anglican Church finds itself today. While once a powerhouse in Australian society drawing energy from its association with the British Empire, offering continued English Culture and spirituality to a wide diaspora of emigrants to Australia and elsewhere. From over 41% of the population in 1921 it has fallen to 13.3% and has a very aged profile of those who identify as Anglicans and even more so for attenders.

This decline began in the 1960s which witnessed the economic withdrawal of The United Kingdom, much cultural change, and the beginnings of the latest wave of global communication. The source of religious legitimacy and cultural power slipped away from the churches. Migration no longer brought new Australians from English and Anglican backgrounds which had fed post-war growth. This has all been analysed, but this is now, the time God has given us to live and the people around us are the people God would have us love.

Loughrey offers an opportunity to reflect on the changes we are called to make in order for the Kingdom of God to grow. A church on the margins has a different role to play than a church of the establishment. The challenge put here is for the church to ask what it means today for it to be genuinely grounded in Australia, drawing on deep Australian spiritualities, but moving forward with eyes focused here and not abroad on some non-existent glorified false memory of what never was.

I found each chapter to be enabling, not complaining, or blaming. The opportunity is given to each to bring their perspective, their wrestling with the issues, not so much to find THE answer as to commence a trusting, risky conversation among faithful people seeking to be their faith today and HERE in Australia.

Professor, The Reverend Gary D. Bouma,
Emeritus Professor Monash University and Associate Priest
St John's East Malvern

Introduction

The following is offered for what it is: the musing of a Vicar in a small suburban parish on a Sunday morning. They are the musings of a community intent upon following and living out the economy of God in a particular place.

What follows is not an academic treatise or an in-depth theological study. There are many others who can and have done such. It is simply an attempt to start a conversation about the pot-plant we in the Anglican Church of Australia, in particular, have inherited.

I first heard this metaphor used at a conference I attended in the middle of 2018. The Reverend Diane Langham introduced this metaphor in her talk to the conference with particular reference to the intersection of colonisers and First Nations people in this country. She was arguing for a new way of being church in Australia that was respectful of what was already here in the dirt under our feet.

In thinking about that metaphor, I began to think about how we hold on to what we have inherited without taking the time to reflect on what it is, where it came from and whether or not it is useful in the place we now find ourselves. As I note in this little book, there is no definitive answer, just a lot of questions, but unless we begin to address the questions, we will continue to live in another place and time disconnected from the wonder and beauty of this place we call Australia.

In writing this book, I wish to acknowledge the sovereign people of this country in which we live, and the elders of all First Nations past, present and emerging.

Glenn Loughrey

Breaking The Sacred Pot

John 6:35-51

[35]*Jesus said to them, 'I am the bread of life. Whoever comes to me will never be hungry, and whoever believes in me will never be thirsty.* [36]*But I said to you that you have seen me and yet do not believe.* [37]*Everything that the Father gives me will come to me, and anyone who comes to me I will never drive away;* [38]*for I have come down from heaven, not to do my own will, but the will of him who sent me.* [39]*And this is the will of him who sent me, that I should lose nothing of all that he has given me, but raise it up on the last day.* [40]*This is indeed the will of my Father, that all who see the Son and believe in him may have eternal life; and I will raise them up on the last day.'* [41]*Then the Jews began to complain about him because he said, 'I am the bread that came down from heaven.'* [42]*They were saying, 'Is not this Jesus, the son of Joseph, whose father and mother we know? How can he now say, "I have come down from heaven"?"* [43]*Jesus answered them, 'Do not complain among yourselves.* [44]*No one can come to me unless drawn by the Father who sent me; and I will raise that person up on the last day.* [45]*It is written in the prophets, 'And they shall all be taught by God.' Everyone who has heard and learned from the Father comes to me.* [46]*Not that anyone has seen the Father except the one who is from God; he has seen the Father.* [47]*Very truly, I tell you, whoever believes has eternal life.* [48]*I am the bread of life.* [49]*Your ancestors ate the manna in the*

wilderness, and they died.[50]*This is the bread that comes down from heaven, so that one may eat of it and not die.* [51]*I am the living bread that came down from heaven. Whoever eats of this bread will live forever; and the bread that I will give for the life of the world is my flesh.'*

***

We are at an interesting time in the history of the Australian church. Much of what we have taken for granted has either been lost or is, at least, being challenged by both modern religious and secular people. The structures we have taken for granted, the language of our liturgy, hymns and theology as well as the role of the church in society are under siege. Even the most recent incarnation of the Prayer Book is now deemed by some academics, clergy and lay people to be insufficient for both the present and future. The same could perhaps be said about the hymnbook.

There is a move for the development of a new prayer book for use in Australia.

I would suggest not only is there a need for such but there needs to be a contextualisation of the church's foundational beliefs, liturgies and language to accommodate its Australian context in the 21st century.

It has been suggested the church in Australia could be likened to a pot plant that grandmother gave you when you moved out of home and into your new place. It came in a beautiful period pot hand made in some famous pottery and valued for both its aesthetic beauty and intrinsic value. You have kept the plant in that pot and taken it with you from house to house and it remains with you today in your retirement. The plant has neither grown nor flourished but it has survived. It is still in the same pot.

It's the pot that matters, not the plant.

The Anglican Church in Australia remains the Church of England, a Northern European Church, despite its name change, because that's the pot it came in and that's the pot we carry around with us from day to day. It is time to either take the plant, the Good News of Jesus Christ, out of the pot or, more dramatically, to knock the pot off its pedestal and allow it to shatter into pieces. If we can collect pieces to reuse, that will be good, but we need to plant the plant into the Australian context, and to do it soon.

John's community is battling with its own unique identity as a people of God, in particular a people who sees Jesus as the Chosen One of God. They are Jews. They have been practising the Jewish faith. This Jewish Rabbi is changing their language and beliefs about the reality of God and they are struggling to work out how that fits with the plant and pot they have been given to cherish. Is the plant really the Son of God and if so, has it outgrown the pot called the Jewish faith? If it is a new planting of the truth in the context of their experience, what are the words and the language one can use to understand it so it makes sense both now and as a continuation of past belief?

This passage is not just about Jesus being the everyday staple that nourishes us physically. That is a literal reading of this text. This statement is more than a metaphor we can use to describe Jesus, and it is not primarily a statement about the Eucharist, although the sacramental element is not far from the centre of this discussion.

In his exposition of this passage, scholar James F. McGrath[1] suggests, 'In this chapter, Jesus is identified as the true manna

---

[1]   "Food For Thought: The Bread of Life Discourse (John 6:25-71) in Johannine Legitimation," by James F. McGrath, from *Theological Gathering 2* (Winter 1997).

or bread from heaven. The origin of this concept is probably the need to show that Jesus fulfilled the Jewish expectation of an eschatological provision of manna, coupled with the developing Wisdom Christology formulated from the need to contrast Jesus with Moses and/or Torah. Although Eucharistic language and imagery does play an important part in this chapter, we have not found the Eucharist to be its central focus. Rather, the bread of life discourse represents a Christological exposition of the Old Testament manna tradition. Eucharistic language is thus probably used not as an end in itself, but because it enables faith in Jesus to be expounded in a way that is relevant to the Johannine community's legitimation of its beliefs and practices in the context of its conflict with the synagogue.'

Context is the key word. Here it refers to the context of disagreement with the synagogue. It is about how they were to make sense of what they believed by reaching back to the Exodus stories and making these stories a fertile ground within their own context in which to flourish and give life.

The Christian church, and in this case the Anglican Church, is being challenged to take its long and hard-fought traditions and to plant them in the soil or context that is Australia, allowing the plant to grow and become, not an import but a native of this place. This is a challenge because no church, even those who perceive they have adapted to attract young people have actually allowed the gospel to grow into an Australian native. They still use images, liturgies, practices birthed in other places ranging from the Middle East, Europe, England, Africa and the Protestant mega churches of the USA.

This is more than making room for Aboriginal spirituality and language for example. While that may be a start, it can be as an appropriation of Aboriginal intellectual property. It is more than gender-neutral language or the adaptation of liturgies to include the LGBTQI communities for baptisms, weddings and funerals. It is more than changing the dove as the symbol of the Holy Spirit to, say, "The white cockatoo". It is more than shifting the church year around so that the images of the seasons actually equate with the season we are in, seeing, in its simplest form, Easter and Christmas transposed.

Planting the plant in the Australian context will require:

- coming to grips with the church's history in this country, coming to grips with the ethos of the space we now inhabit;
- coming to grips with the language and spirituality of this context
- coming to grips with the need to mature both as a nation and as a church – growing up as a people into our own identity.

Each of these could occupy a paper on its own so there is no doubt that this is and will be a challenge, and it is the challenge John's Jesus addresses in this discourse on 'I am the bread of life'.

If we are serious about being the church for the 21st century and beyond, we owe it to ourselves, to all who have gone before us and all still to come to address these questions. It is one of the driving factors behind our parish's strategic plan[2]. As we begin to attract new people, engage with new people and work with new people, we will realise that we have to begin to take the plant, Jesus, out of the pot that came from England on the First Fleet and plant it in the land of the Werrundjeri people of the Kulin nations and see what happens.

This is not a chapter with a nice little wrap up. It's a chapter with a challenge. What church are you going to leave behind: the one you have carefully nourished in the pot or one that comes into being because you take the plant, Jesus, out of the pot and plant him here and now? This must be an ongoing discussion for the church in Australia.

---

2   St Oswald's Anglican Church, Diocese of Melbourne. This parish has developed a professional strategic plan to oversight its engagement and contextualisation of the church's message to the community.

History

John 6:51-58

[51]*'I am the living bread that came down from heaven. Whoever eats of this bread will live forever; and the bread that I will give for the life of the world is my flesh.'* [52]*The Jews then disputed among themselves, saying, 'How can this man give us his flesh to eat?'* [53]*So Jesus said to them, 'Very truly, I tell you, unless you eat the flesh of the Son of Man and drink his blood, you have no life in you.* [54]*Those who eat my flesh and drink my blood have eternal life, and I will raise them up on the last day;* [55]*for my flesh is true food and my blood is true drink.* [56]*Those who eat my flesh and drink my blood abide in me, and I in them.* [57]*Just as the living Father sent me, and I live because of the Father, so whoever eats me will live because of me.* [58]*This is the bread that came down from heaven, not like that which your ancestors ate, and they died. But the one who eats this bread will live forever.'*

***

At the end of the service in which I introduced this topic, I was challenged to further explore what it may look like to do that within the Australian context.

In the last chapter, we began to look at the bread of life discourse in the context of John's community and its conflict with the traditional Jewish understanding of God, particularly the manna of heaven their ancestors received in the wilderness.

I suggested this passage is not primarily about the Eucharist but a language and ritual based attempt to place Jesus as the Chosen One within their experience and the understanding of God they had received from their tradition.

I commented that the Anglican Church and all that comes with it came to us from another context and relied on language, liturgy, traditions and practices foreign to this context, Australia. We should also recognise that the place of the church in society is no longer the same as it was when it was transplanted here.

I suggested suggested four points to be considered:

- coming to grips with the church's history in this country;
- coming to grips with the ethos of the space
  we now inhabit;
- coming to grips with the language and spirituality
  of this context
- coming to grips with the need to mature both as a nation
  and as a church.

Here I will comment briefly on the first of these:

- coming to grips with the church's history in this country;

John's Jesus states: 'I am the living bread that came down from heaven. Whoever eats of this bread will live forever; and the bread that I will give for the life of the world is my flesh.' The word *living* is important to our discussion. Living can be understood as the normal process of life – birth, childhood, maturation and death. It is the process of becoming and growing in wisdom and knowledge; and the implementing of experience in new and previously un-experienced ways. It is how we now understand Jesus. He didn't come into the world a completed being; he became the person he was in relation to the world in which he lived – his context. The implication here is that while he always remains the divine manna, it will be experienced and lived in ever-changing ways within the context of our lives. It is not finished.

This also refers to the way the church engages with its context. While, based on history, we can acknowledge the changing nature and role of church in society since Arthur Phillip arrived, and acknowledge that that history is a mix of good, not so good and very not so good outcomes, two significant events in the last few years have significantly impacted on the place and privilege of the church in general and the Anglican Church in particular.

The first was the *Royal Commission into Institutional Child Abuse*[3] and the second was the *Statement from the Heart*[4] enacted by First Nations People. These two events have changed the landscape for the church and shifted the balance of power out of the hands of the institution and into the hands of the general public, especially, in these cases, the victims of the failures of these institutions.

In the first case, it has deeply damaged the reputation of the church and now requires mandated reparation. The fact that some Dioceses have said they will be selling property to pay redress signifies the financial impact. The continuing public discussion, rightly or wrongly, over such as the position of Bishop Hollingworth[5] and others implicated in the failure adds to the pressure being applied. The move by the former tax office head Terry Hamilton[6] to write to the Prime Minister and the head of the charities commission requesting that the tax benefits and charity status of those organisations who failed to protect children be denied as they have failed to comply with the basic

---

3   Royal Commission into Institutional Responses to Child Sexual Abuse, 2013 –2017; www.childabuseroyalcommission.gov.au

4   Uluru Statement from the Heart www.referendumcouncil.org.au/sites/default/files/2017-05/Uluru_Statement_From_The_Heart_0.PDF

5   Anglican Church faces complaints over Peter Hollingworth remaining a bishop. http://www.abc.net.au/news/2018-08-08/abuse-survivors-outraged-that-hollingworth-remains-a-bishop/10086910

6   Churches should lose charity status over child abuse, former tax official says, www.theguardian.com/australia-news/2018/aug/13/churches-should-lose-charity-status-over-child-abuse-former-tax-head-says

requirements of the legislation raises further questions for the future of the church as we know it.

As a result of the most significant Australia-wide, community based consultation on any constitutional issue resulting in a pan-Aboriginal statement on constitutional change, the *Statement of the Heart*, Aboriginal people no longer see themselves as powerless. This twelve month long process of consulting widely with the Aboriginal community (twelve consultations) resulted in the ratifying of the decisions made at each of those consultations. Aboriginal people realised the importance of the task and put aside personal and clan concerns to invite the Australian people to join them on the road to unity and reconciliation. They understand, by the responses of governments and churches, that the balance of power has shifted and that they are now have a voice. The rapid steps taken by the government at the highest levels to shutdown the invitation from the First Nations Peoples are not evidence of power but of the weakness of the Australian constitutional sovereignty, stolen as it was from those whose sovereignty has never been ceded.

In relation to the church, a movement has been developing alongside the process toward the statement, to call the churches and other institutions to account for their actions in the past and the privileges gained from the colonisation of this country. This movement of senior Aboriginal elders, lawyers and academics will be seeking treaty, truth-telling and reparation and it won't be satisfied with terms set by the church. This has gathered momentum as a result of the statement by the Bishop of Tasmania that churches will be sold for redress for victims of child abuse[7].

These are serious challenges, along with falling attendance, ageing congregations and the increasing disengagement with the institutional church in favour of spirituality and more, asking us to reimagine faith and practice, mindful of the Spirits

---

7   'Historic' day as Tasmanian Anglican Church votes to sell 76 church buildings; www.examiner.com.au/story/5444222/historic-day-as-anglican-church-votes-to-sell-76-church-buildings/

continuing call to renewal. We can no longer rely on what we previously understood about faith and the Divine. We can no longer rely on an outdated understanding of God's interaction in the world and that the church, we, are the ones who hold the keys to that relationship. As a result of the living bread coming into the world, the whole of the world has been impregnated with the spirit of justice and hope and we are to find ways to cooperate with it.

The church has lived through and been transformed by challenges as impactive as these in previous centuries. The reformation, counter reformation, the to and fro over the future of the English church in the Middle Ages and more give us hope. The church was able to ride out those challenges and be changed and transformed by them. God's grace is sufficient for our context but we must not attempt to avoid the challenging questions put to us in our particular context.

This modern-day call comes in the voices of those both outside and within the church who want us to live up to our stated relationship with God. In other words, to make real what we say we believe, in a new time and place.

How do we do that?

- by accepting that we who make up the church are human and make mistakes, that how we understand others and the world is constantly changing and what we once thought was appropriate no longer is.

- by accepting that we have to share the revelation of Divine wisdom with others who are not part of our faith or denomination. We no longer own it exclusively.

- by accepting that our place in the world has shrunk in terms of our ability to influence the nation state in that we no longer sit at its centre. Paradoxically, our place in the world has expanded as a result as it allows us the opportunity to work with other like-minded people to bring about the justice of God for all.

We are living in a stage of faith development that is becoming more and more democratic – all are included in the kingdom of justice and all have the right to a say in how that kingdom is revealed and how they individually engage with that kingdom.

'I am the living bread that came down from heaven. Whoever eats of this bread will live forever; and the bread that I will give for the life of the world is my flesh.'

Jesus leaves us in no doubt that becoming the manna from heaven is a costly process; we will not be left untouched in our humanity. Not even the church will be left untouched. Becoming a church for the Australian context will see us giving our living self to be consumed and transformed into a new way of being the kingdom of justice in this place called Australia.

It will be costly but it also has the potential to bring great rewards.

Ethos

John 6:56-69

⁶'Those who eat my flesh and drink my blood abide in me, and I in them.⁵⁷Just as the living Father sent me, and I live because of the Father, so whoever eats me will live because of me. ⁵⁸This is the bread that came down from heaven, not like that which your ancestors ate, and they died. But the one who eats this bread will live forever.' ⁵⁹He said these things while he was teaching in the synagogue at Capernaum.

Ephesians 6:10-20

¹⁰Finally, be strong in the Lord and in the strength of his power. ¹¹Put on the whole armour of God, so that you may be able to stand against the wiles of the devil. ¹²For our struggle is not against enemies of blood and flesh, but against the rulers, against the authorities, against the cosmic powers of this present darkness, against the spiritual forces of evil in the heavenly places. ¹³Therefore take up the whole armour of God, so that you may be able to withstand on that evil day, and having done everything, to stand firm. ¹⁴Stand therefore, and fasten the belt of truth around your waist, and put on the breastplate of righteousness. ¹⁵As shoes for your feet put on whatever will make you ready to proclaim the gospel of peace. ¹⁶With all of these, take the shield of faith, with which you will be

able to quench all the flaming arrows of the evil one. [17]Take the helmet of salvation, and the sword of the Spirit, which is the word of God. [18]Pray in the Spirit at all times in every prayer and supplication. To that end keep alert and always persevere in supplication for all the saints.

[19]Pray also for me, so that when I speak, a message may be given to me to make known with boldness the mystery of the gospel, [20]for which I am an ambassador in chains. Pray that I may declare it boldly, as I must speak.

***

We continue our exploration of the pot and the plant and the process of transplanting the faith narrative we received from Western Europe into the Australian context. In the last chapter, we looked at the need to come to grips with the church's history in this country and we ended with three realistically positive statements:

- by accepting that we who make up the church are human and make mistakes, that how we understand others and the world is constantly changing and what we once thought was appropriate no longer is.

- by accepting that we have to share the revelation of Divine wisdom with others who are not part of our faith or denomination, we no longer own it exclusively.

- by accepting that our place in the world has shrunk in that we no longer sit at its centre, but paradoxically, by doing so, our place in the world has expanded as we work with other like-minded people to bring about the justice of God for all.

- coming to grips with the ethos of the space
we now inhabit.

Now we will look at the second of the four original statements of process:

- What is the social and religious atmosphere in which we live and how do we respond to what we discover?

In John's Gospel and the accompanying Ephesians Epistle, John and the Pauline tradition lay out a challenging landscape for us. The author reminds us that we will need all of our spiritual wiles and tools to live and become whole in what Ephesians plainly sees as a hostile environment. He is writing from his own experience and the hostility he has met from both the Jewish and non-Jewish worldviews. He seems to say that we will need to be on the defensive if we are going to survive; and that the tools he outlines in this passage are essential for that purpose. Traditionally, we have interpreted this passage as ways of self-protection, of the protection of our gift of eternal life from the sin of backsliding or turning away.

This is our legacy from the pot plant – we have to protect what we have from the environment, the space in which we find ourselves; otherwise the plant, in this case our faith, will die.

What if there is another way to see this?

Is he, in fact, saying to us that these are the tools we need to engage with as we analyse the ethos or atmosphere in which we live? These are not so much defensive tools but tools of engagement, tools which – if we employ them appropriately – will allow us to stay fully aware of what is happening around us and how to respond, grow and be transformed by it.

The John reading is also blunt and direct. David Lose suggests '...the picture St John draws for us in today's reading may not a pretty one, but it is a rather realistic one. It is, in other words, a fairly accurate portrait of disbelief, with Jesus surrounded by folks who wanted to believe, who used to believe, who have been trying to believe, but have gone through the motions too long and have finally given up.[8] I suspect this is an accurate reading of where we are in our own time and space.

Jesus is surrounded by people who are seeking a new deal with life, a new deal with faith and for the future. They want to be recognised and heard by those in power, both secular and religious. They have heard the same old platitudes of faithfulness required from them and inherent in God's part of the deal and have come to the conclusion, with Tom Waits, that 'God's away on business'[9]. They have been waiting for their faith to be rewarded, for the promises of God to be received and the violence of everyday life to cease. They have been disappointed so many times that they have decided they have had enough and moved away. Others have stayed but they are half-hearted and cynical and still others are fervent and intense but deep down unsure of whether this story of the covenant relationship with God and/or Jesus is the real deal.

Does this sound familiar? Perhaps you can see yourself somewhere in this mix? I would be surprised if you didn't. I do. This is the harshness of faith – the now and then of what we believe – we believe it *now* but we are waiting for *then* to experience it – whereever then may be.

Is this not the ethos of the society the church is in the midst of at this time and place?

The growing number of people identifying as nones – those without any religious affiliation – is a sign of the move away from traditional religion in search of something different or, in some cases, nothing at all. The success of books such as *The God Delusion* by Richard Dawkins[10], the rise of the humanist church of such as Alain de Botton and the simple

---

8   http://www.davidlose.net/2015/08/pentecost-13-b/

9   "God's Away on Business", "Blood Money", 2002, Tom Waits and Kathleen Brennan

10   Dawkins, R. (2006). The God delusion. Boston: Houghton Mifflin Co..

'not knowing anything about God and Jesus' of much of the younger generation signifies the groups Lose referred to within the quoted passage.

Since the enlightenment and the rise of the individual as the centre of all that is, and the subsequent reduction of people to the single most important identity they have – that of individual economic units or consumers – the influence of religion has been reduced to just another consumer product.

In Australia, this has been our history. The initial colonisation of this country was primarily by those who, for various reasons, were assigned to a penal colony as the means to rid England's jails of overcrowding and to achieve, primarily, a new economic endeavour. They came with little or no religious guidance in the first instance, and were left to their own imaginations to create meaning in the new world.

The church became visibly a middle/upper class institution to which one belonged without necessarily having faith or knowing what that looked like. This, arguably, remained the case up until relatively recently. The arrival, first, of Irish Catholics and then the faith and religions of European migrants after the two world wars continued the apparent nominal Christian ethos. This changed again with the official ending of the White Australian policy[11] and the arrival of Asian, Middle Eastern and African immigrants since the 1970s.

Australia is now caught somewhere between the nominal Christian space and the more fervent and diverse faith experiences of new immigrants and the individual search for meaning through such phenomena as meditation, mindfulness and the faiths and practices which support such. Nominal Christianity has also been impacted by the history of the church we referred to previously. In addition, we have the cost and process of home ownership and home-making vastly different

11   http://www.nma.gov.au/online_features/defining_moments/featured/white_ australia_policy_begins

from that of the 1950s and 60s, seeming to delay interest in existential 'things' until much later in life. For most there simply isn't the time or the financial freedom to engage, as was the case previously. Today, for example, it is suggested the average age of becoming a member of the Anglican Church is sixty. This is not a sign that religion is of consequence only for older people, but recognises that only after having completed family and career responsibilities do people have time for things of religion.

While this is a superficial reading of the signs of the time, the climate and ethos has changed and we are unsure of how to respond.

Alyce McKenzie asks, 'The question arises that if we are no longer going about with him, then where are we going?'[12]

We can only answer this question for ourselves. We cannot answer it for others. Like the remnant in John's Gospel can we answer with Peter, 'Lord, to whom can we go? You have the words of eternal life. We have come to believe and know that you are the Holy One of God.'

The key word here is 'come'. We recognise we have not always believed but through a process of living we have come to this place.

In the midst of the diverse landscape that is modern Australia, we are to leave space for others to come to faith in the same way. And, remember, this will not be the majority, but as John's Jesus lays out clearly, it may only be a remnant and that's okay.

---

12   http://www.patheos.com/progressive-christian/jesus-journey-and-ours-alyce-mckenzie-08-20-2012.html

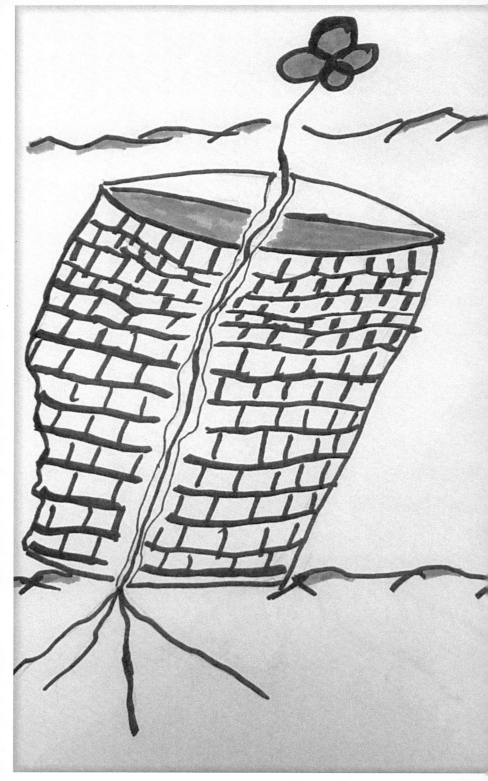

Language and Spirituality

Mark 7:1-23

Now when the Pharisees and some of the scribes who had come from Jerusalem gathered around him, [2]they noticed that some of his disciples were eating with defiled hands, that is, without washing them.[3](For the Pharisees, and all the Jews, do not eat unless they thoroughly wash their hands, thus observing the tradition of the elders; [4]and they do not eat anything from the market unless they wash it; and there are also many other traditions that they observe, the washing of cups, pots, and bronze kettles.) [5]So the Pharisees and the scribes asked him, 'Why do your disciples not live according to the tradition of the elders, but eat with defiled hands?' [6]He said to them, 'Isaiah prophesied rightly about you hypocrites, as it is written,

> *"This people honours me with their lips, but their hearts are far from me; [7]in vain do they worship me, teaching human precepts as doctrines."*
>
> [8]*You abandon the commandment of God and hold to human tradition.'*

[9]*Then he said to them, 'You have a fine way of rejecting the commandment of God in order to keep your tradition! [10]For Moses said, 'Honor your father and your mother'; and, 'Whoever speaks evil of father or mother must surely die.' [11]But you say that if anyone tells father or mother, 'Whatever support you might have had from me is Corban' (that is, an offering to God)— [12]then you no longer permit doing anything for a father or mother, [13]thus making void the word of God through your tradition that you have handed on. And you do many things like this.'*

[14]*Then he called the crowd again and said to them, 'Listen to me, all of you, and understand:* [15]*there is nothing outside a person that by going in can defile, but the things that come out are what defile.'*

[17]*When he had left the crowd and entered the house, his disciples asked him about the parable.* [18]*He said to them, 'Then do you also fail to understand? Do you not see that whatever goes into a person from outside cannot defile,* [19]*since it enters, not the heart but the stomach, and goes out into the sewer?' (Thus he declared all foods clean.)* [20]*And he said, 'It is what comes out of a person that defiles.* [21]*For it is from within, from the human heart, that evil intentions come: fornication, theft, murder,* [22]*adultery, avarice, wickedness, deceit, licentiousness, envy, slander, pride, folly.* [23]*All these evil things come from within, and they defile a person.'*

James 1:17-27

[17]*Every generous act of giving, with every perfect gift, is from above, coming down from the Father of lights, with whom there is no variation or shadow due to change.* [18]*In fulfilment of his own purpose he gave us birth by the word of truth, so that we would become a kind of first fruits of his creatures.*

[19]*You must understand this, my beloved: let everyone be quick to listen, slow to speak, slow to anger;* [20]*for your anger does not produce God's righteousness.* [21]*Therefore rid yourselves of all sordidness and rank growth of wickedness, and welcome with meekness the implanted word that has the power to save your souls.* [22]*But be doers of the word, and not merely hearers who deceive themselves.* [23]*For if any are hearers of the word and not doers, they are like those who look at themselves in a mirror;* [24]*for they look at themselves and, on going away, immediately forget what they were like.* [25]*But those who look into the perfect law,*

the law of liberty, and persevere, being not hearers who forget but doers who act—they will be blessed in their doing. [26] If any think they are religious, and do not bridle their tongues but deceive their hearts, their religion is worthless. [27] Religion that is pure and undefiled before God, the Father, is this: to care for orphans and widows in their distress, and to keep oneself unstained by the world.

***

It is now time to focus on the third of our four points reflecting on the pot and the plant in the Australian context:

- Coming to grips with the language and spirituality.

Recently, I went to see the Brett Whitely/David Baldesean[13] exhibition at the National Gallery of Victoria, Federation Square.

What struck me about both these exemplary Australian artists and their works – because they are quintessentially Australian – is their sensuous brutality deeply fixated with the human engagement with place. The majority of their works contain distorted human, female bodies, with small heads and painted in the palette of the Australian outback. Even Whitley's landscapes embraced the female shape in browns and ochres and many of the works were made to seem unfinished, as if a battle had been fought and lost. The female form suggests hope in fecundity and fertility that is primal and primary, unlike the mind which is of little consequence. You cannot outthink this place; you can only become like it. The early deaths of both artists may be seen to suggest they lost that battle.

The feminist theologian, Elizabeth Johnson, asserts that language acts – what we say and think becomes actuality in

---

13   www.thecultureconcept.com/baldessinwhiteley-parallel-visions-showcased-ngv-australia

our daily living. We are not distant from the language we use to describe the act of being in the context of our lives, even the language of art

Both James and Mark reflect on this in the context of religious thought and practice. For Mark's Jesus, the way language is used to justify acts designed not for the fulfillment of religious obligation but for the fulfillment of personal gain is an abomination. The result of such language is that those for whom the obligation was designed to protect in fact are the victims of the language. Specifically, Jesus is using the case of parental or elder abuse as a result of so called pious behaviour by their children – what was for you I have already given to the Lord, so there is nothing else for you.

He goes on to attack the idea of clean and unclean, righteous and unrighteous. He asserts physical food does not bring about bad behaviour, the language and thought that comes from within does. It is our language and religious ethos that results in inappropriate behaviour towards others, especially those who are marginalised and isolated.

James continues this concept. For him, your actions must be in line with what you say you believe. It is no good committing to a set of beliefs if you simply don't do that when the chips are down, where the rubber meets the road.

The difficulty both address is the blindness one has to ones own biases and failures to be what you say you are. There is a story told about one of the Ancient Desert Fathers, Abba Moses. It goes like this:

'A certain brother committed an offence in Scete, the camp of the monks, and when a congregation was assembled [on this matter, they sent after Abba Moses, but he refused to come; then they sent the priest of the church to him, [saying, "Come, for all the people are expecting you," and he rose up and came. He took a basket with a hole in it [and filled it with sand, and carried it upon his shoulders, and those who went out to meet him said

unto him, "What [does this mean, O father?" And he said to them, "The sands are my sins which are running down behind me and I [cannot see them, and, even, have come to this day to judge shortcomings which are not mine." And when they heard [this they set free that brother and said nothing further to him.[14]

Mark, James and Abba Moses all point to the following in terms of spiritual ethos and language:

- be doers –
- be fair dinkum –
- be fair – fair go
- be in tune with nature
- listen to land/country –

Sounds like what we say we believe as Australians? These ideals are often given as the values of this country, values that make us different to others. And in some ways this is true.

In talking to Australians (not politicians, shock jocks or propagandists), there is a genuine sense that these are values, both practical and spiritual, sitting at the centre of who we are. We genuinely believe these reflect how we think, speak and act, and my experience of Australians in communities I have lived in, primarily confirm this.

We are a country with deep respect for the land and those who work on it and perhaps it could be said to be similar to the way Aboriginal people do. When those on the land are in trouble because of the vagaries of nature, we rally around the romantic view we have of them. Yet there is a difference. Aboriginal people traditionally lived in harmony with the land, allowing it to speak into their lives; we tend to want to overcome, usurp the land to make it profitable and a servant of our economic agenda. The language we use reinforces this and shifts our relationship from unity to duality – us against nature.

---

14 https://lacopts.org/story/sayings-of-the-strong-saint-abba-moses/

We do believe in being doers, but not doers that necessarily put our words into practice out of compassion but to do so to avoid being leaners. He/she is a self-made man/women is still a compliment we all seek. Doing is still deeply embedded in the Protestant work ethic and those without work, including retirees, are seen as leaners to be given only what is necessary to stave off the elements but no more. The counter to this is the ditty written by Michael Leunig:

'What is worth doing and what is worth having?' asks Vasco of his friend Mr. Curly.

'It is worth doing nothing and it is worth having a rest', advises the sagacious Mr. Curly. 'In spite of all the difficulty it may cause, you MUST rest, Vasco – otherwise you will become RESTLESS!'[15]

We do want people to be fair dinkum and to tell it like it is, as long as that aligns with our understanding of what the truth is. We struggle to engage in discussions that change and transform us. Like those around Abba Moses, we are unable to see when we ourselves are not fair dinkum, when what we say and do does not align with what we say we believe.

Perhaps the issue is how to come to grips, not so much with the language and spirituality, but with the split between what we have been told is the essence of language and spirituality and the reality embedded in the rhetoric of our national myths: how the country was settled, the formation of the Federation, the ANZAC and military hero legend, the fair and honourable sports person, the continuing white Australian paranoia, denial of our treatment of the original inhabitants of this country, and more. What do these say about how we believe and speak?

This is the challenge found in the Mark and James readings. Neither gives a quick answer but lays down for their

15   The Curly Pyjama Letters Michael Leunig ISBN: 9780143005469 | | Release 2006 Penguin Australia

listeners what it looks like from a distance – their rhetoric and purported spirituality is lacking in substance.

The Australian scene is further complicated but the growing cynicism about anything those who are the custodians of our language and spirituality have to say. They do not trust the church to do the right thing and definitely take anything that comes from our political leaders with a tonne of salt. As they saw in the 2018 change of Prime Minister, the more things change the more they stays the same. Those who came here on the first fleet were just as cynical on both accounts.

Perhaps what we have as the primary spiritual ethos in this county is cynicism calling us who purport to speak for the Divine to ensure that we actually believe what we say –

- that all are equal, regardless of status, class, nationality, gender identification and more;
- that all are welcome in this country and given a fair go;
- that we begin to treat the land we live on as a soul mate and not a means to an economic end and
- to remember that in many ways we are complicit in bringing this cynicism into being by our past and continuing failure to marry spirituality and language with action.

These are not guarantees of resolving the issue but unless we live up to our language and purported spiritual ethos, the chances are others won't bother to either.

Maturity

James 2:1-17

My brothers and sisters, do you with your acts of favouritism really believe in our glorious Lord Jesus Christ? [2]*For if a person with gold rings and in fine clothes comes into your assembly, and if a poor person in dirty clothes also comes in,* [3]*and if you take notice of the one wearing the fine clothes and say, 'Have a seat here, please,' while to the one who is poor you say, 'Stand there,' or, 'Sit at my feet,'* [4]*have you not made distinctions among yourselves, and become judges with evil thoughts?* [5]*Listen, my beloved brothers and sisters. Has not God chosen the poor in the world to be rich in faith and to be heirs of the kingdom that he has promised to those who love him?* [6]*But you have dishonoured the poor. Is it not the rich who oppress you? Is it not they who drag you into court?* [7]*Is it not they who blaspheme the excellent name that was invoked over you?*

[8]*You do well if you really fulfil the royal law according to the scripture, 'You shall love your neighbour as yourself.'* [9]*But if you show partiality, you commit sin and are convicted by the law as transgressors.* [10]*For whoever keeps the whole law but fails in one point has become accountable for all of it.* [11]*For the one who said, 'You shall not commit adultery,' also said, 'You shall not murder.' Now if you do not commit adultery but if you murder, you have become a transgressor of the law.* [12]*So speak and so act as those who are to be judged by the law of liberty.* 13*For judgment will be without mercy to anyone who has shown no mercy; mercy triumphs over judgment.*

[14]*What good is it, my brothers and sisters, if you say you have faith but do not have works? Can faith save you?* [15]*If a brother or sister is naked and lacks daily food,* [16]*and one of you says to them, 'Go in peace; keep warm and eat your fill,' and yet you do*

not supply their bodily needs, what is the good of that? [17] *So faith by itself, if it has no works, is dead.*

Mark 7:24-37

From there he set out and went away to the region of Tyre. He entered a house and did not want anyone to know he was there. Yet he could not escape notice, [25] *but a woman whose little daughter had an unclean spirit immediately heard about him, and she came and bowed down at his feet.* [26] *Now the woman was a Gentile, of Syrophoenician origin. She begged him to cast the demon out of her daughter.* [27] *He said to her, 'Let the children be fed first, for it is not fair to take the children's food and throw it to the dogs.'* [28] *But she answered him, 'Sir, even the dogs under the table eat the children's crumbs.'* [29] *Then he said to her, 'For saying that, you may go—the demon has left your daughter.'* [30] *So she went home, found the child lying on the bed, and the demon gone.*

[31] *Then he returned from the region of Tyre, and went by way of Sidon towards the Sea of Galilee, in the region of the Decapolis.* [32] *They brought to him a deaf man who had an impediment in his speech; and they begged him to lay his hand on him.* [33] *He took him aside in private, away from the crowd, and put his fingers into his ears, and he spat and touched his tongue.* [34] *Then looking up to heaven, he sighed and said to him, 'Ephphatha,' that is, 'Be opened.'* [35] *And immediately his ears were opened, his tongue was released, and he spoke plainly.* [36] *Then Jesus ordered them to tell no one; but the more he ordered them, the more zealously they proclaimed it.* [37] *They were astounded beyond measure, saying, 'He has done everything well; he even makes the deaf to hear and the mute to speak.'*

***

Now we turn to the last of the four focal points in relation to the pot and the plant.

- Coming to grips with the need to mature both as a nation and as a church.

This is a complex and problematic topic. How can we approach this question without insinuating that somehow, something is wrong with both the nation and the church? What does it mean to be mature in both arenas and what does it look like not to be mature?

It is all about identity and how we see ourselves and whether or not how we see ourselves sustains our authentic selves without the need to appeal to others (nations or ideologies) to affirm us. It involves the self-assurance that we are ok despite consisting of all the human failings any institution will experience. Why? Because we, nation and church, are made up of the general public and that makes us problematic at best.

Are we able to look ourselves in the mirror and say, collectively that we are okay; not perfect, not without great errors of judgment, ill-informed practice, outdated world views or unexplainable fears, but okay? Are we able to own our past, our biases, our prejudices, our 'isms and be okay about them, seeking to be transformed in such a way that these no longer reign supreme in our psyche?

Maturity places us where we understand that what we wished for, what we were told and who we are, are three completely different experiences. We are mature when we are comfortable with who we are and can speak and act out of that place. This happens when we no longer blame others for failing us because they told us stuff that didn't come true; it happens when we put aside what we wished for in childish hope; it happens when we are okay with the disparity between these and the reality we experience everyday.

When we are okay with that, we are beginning to mature and own our own story in ways that empowers us.

This is the challenge for us as a nation – to own our past (how we became a nation and how we treated the First Nations People), our biases (white Australia policy), our fears (boat people and refugees), our aloneness (the need for a mother – UK; or a big brother – USA), our struggle with cutting our ties with England (becoming a republic) and more. These are questions we have been afraid to answer out of fear of what will happen if... Yet we know from recent events such as giving First Nations People the vote, welcoming Vietnamese boat people, welcoming refugees, embracing multiculturalism, granting marriage equality that the sky has not fallen and neither will it if we stand up and address these and other issues.

These issues are not dissimilar to those faced by the church. It too has to address its past, make a break from the English church, address its blindness to systemic failures, include LGBTQI, disabled, homeless and others; and make a decision to be Australian in Australia. Again, these may seem deeply challenging but we know that despite the warnings, the church has not collapsed because it ordains women or because it has been forced to face the child abuse scandal. The roofs of all churches will not fall in if we begin to mature so that we let go of our preconceived theological and structural positions and listen to the Great Creator Spirit in this land of the Dreaming.

In Mark's Gospel, two people, Jesus and a Gentile woman of Syrophoenician origin, have a public and frank confrontation. They were as different as chalk and cheese in terms of race, as was Jesus and the man he next meets. Lamar Williamson, Jr. (Mark, Interpretation) connects these texts with verses 1-23 with, 'If in the preceding passage Jesus "declared all foods clean" (7:19), in these stories he declares all persons clean, whether a Gentile woman in a pagan city or a man of indeterminate race in the unclean territory of the Decapolis. The stories are two examples of the same principle: Both advance Jesus' repudiation of traditional taboos (p. 137).' [16]

'The racial and religious differences between Jesus and the Gentile woman are unchanged. But what has changed is that courage and caring for a daughter have been shown to be acceptable to God - even when they come from a Gentile heart; even when they come from a woman's heart; even when they come from the heart of a woman who has publicly shamed herself by being out alone, by speaking to a man, and by daring to speak back to a man.' (David Ewart, 2012.)[17]

In this scenario, who is the more mature, who is the one who is most fully aware of themselves and their shortcomings in this confrontation, but believes so strongly in what has to be said that they say it firmly and with deep conviction? On the surface, it's not Jesus.

It's the woman. She is mature enough to know what the situation is and what she wants and that she deserves to get what is right. She will not bow to racism, clericalism, gender power or imputed shame. She is okay and therefore it is okay to be here, now and say what has to be said.

Jesus responds with affirmation, you are okay. All are included in this kingdom, no matter what labels or biases society puts on you or in your way.

Reflecting on the James reading, Daniel B. Clendenin suggests, 'We judge, discriminate, and play favourites for many reasons - race, religion, gender, intelligence, politics, and nationality all come to mind. James uses the example of Christians who favoured the rich over the poor.'[18]

'James wasn't telling the church to be good to the poor and thereby earn salvation. He was saying that if their faith

---

16   http://www.crossmarks.com/brian/mark7x24.htm

17   http://www.holytextures.com/2012/09/mark-7-24-37-year-b-pentecost-september-4-september-10-proper-18-ordinary-23.html

18   https://www.journeywithjesus.net/Essays/20120903JJ.shtml

was genuine, they'd actually be loving their neighbours as themselves.' (Rick Morley, 2012.)[19]

Maturity is the strength to engage with the unknown without the need for assurance that all will be well. It is the ability to address past errors and mistakes and own the responsibility for putting right the future. It is the capacity to hear another out with resorting to fear, ideology or dog-whistle politics. It is the capacity to make the changes necessary for a worthwhile future for all.

The woman and Jesus engage in such a transaction where both are visibly different as a result but neither is diminished. Both grow in stature and in their own understanding of who they are.

The challenge for both the church and the nation is to face the fear of losing what we have or have been privileged to have, to let go of the past and all its warm fuzzy memories and face what is required of us in this new world. A mature nation and church will embrace modern thought, science and practice. It will announce itself confident in its identity in this place, letting go of the need for crutches from another era. We will become inclusive of the diverseness of creation in terms of peoples, faiths, practices, genders, disabilities and races.

The key to this is an educated populace who refuse to be spoken down to by those in power and, like the woman in our story, say, 'Enough. We are here. Take us seriously. Seriously.'

---

19   http://www.rickmorley.com/archives/1900

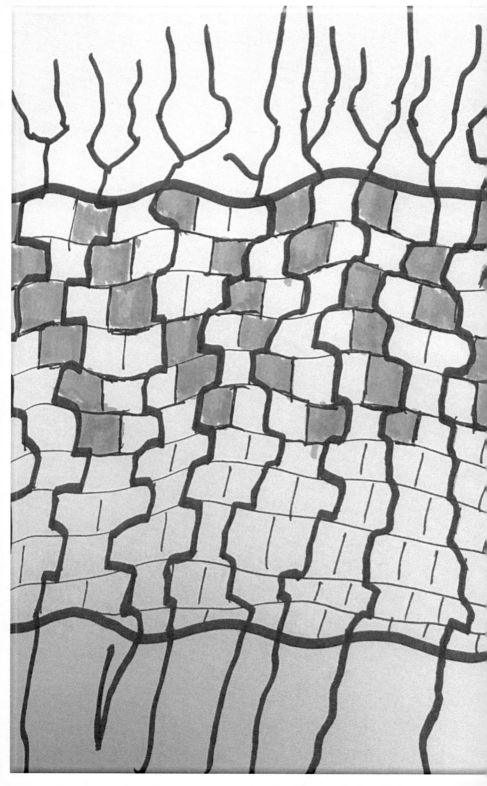

Transformation

Mark 8:27-38

Jesus went on with his disciples to the villages of Caesarea Philippi; and on the way he asked his disciples, 'Who do people say that I am?' [28]*And they answered him, 'John the Baptist; and others, Elijah; and still others, one of the prophets.'* [29]*He asked them, 'But who do you say that I am?' Peter answered him, 'You are the Messiah.'* [30]*And he sternly ordered them not to tell anyone about him.*

[31]*Then he began to teach them that the Son of Man must undergo great suffering, and be rejected by the elders, the chief priests, and the scribes, and be killed, and after three days rise again.* [32]*He said all this quite openly. And Peter took him aside and began to rebuke him.* [33]*But turning and looking at his disciples, he rebuked Peter and said, 'Get behind me, Satan! For you are setting your mind not on divine things but on human things.'*

[34]*He called the crowd with his disciples, and said to them, 'If any want to become my followers, let them deny themselves and take up their cross and follow me.* [35]*For those who want to save their life will lose it, and those who lose their life for my sake, and for the sake of the gospel, will save it.* [36]*For what will it profit them to gain the whole world and forfeit their life?* [37]*Indeed, what can they give in return for their life?* [38]*Those who are ashamed of me and of my words in this adulterous and sinful generation, of them the Son of Man will also be ashamed when he comes in the glory of his Father with the holy angels.'*

***

Time for a recap. We have been exploring the metaphor of a faith and culture transported to this country from Western Europe in grandma's beloved pot. Initially, we raised the question of how do we contextualise that faith and culture by taking it out of our pot.

We suggested that there were four key ideas to be addressed and we undertook the task of exploring each one:

- coming to grips with the church's history in this country;
- coming to grips with the ethos of the space we now inhabit;
- coming to grips with the language and spirituality of this context
- coming to grips with the need to mature both as a nation and as a church.

Now we come to bring this discussion to a pause, not a conclusion, as a result of this passage from Mark's Gospel. It is important to understand this discussion has no fixed point on which to conclude. In fact, it is an ongoing discussion with many unanswered questions, concerns and conundrums to be tackled in our journey into wholeness.

I hope that what we have discussed has raised some interest and that we will find ways to discuss, agree, disagree and move forward, for to stay looking longingly at the pot is to stay trapped in the past, unable to enjoy the immense possibilities available to us today.

In Mark's Gospel, this longing is what Jesus addresses. He says it is time to take the plant out of the pot and put it in the ground where it will do its best work. While it is traditionally understood that this is the moment that Jesus speaks to his disciples about his crucifixion, it could also be seen as the moment he breaks the truth to them about how their worldview, the pot, will be shattered.

It is no longer an intellectual or academic process. It is no longer about theological discussions, miracles or healings. It is no longer about an exciting life-style with this disturbing Rabbi who seems to break all the accepted laws and rules. It is no longer about something that might happen somewhere far off in the future.

It is about *now* and moving into direct confrontation with the powers at loose in the world. It is about taking what you believe and planting it in the soil of relationships and community and watching it be shaken and broken by the winds of fear.

Karoline Lewis suggests 'To 'deny yourself and take up your cross' invites us into what the cross can also mean – not just death and suffering, but God choosing human relationships.'[20] God chose human relationships within a particular context and engaged fully in the pros and cons of human life. This was not an experience that was rarefied and controlled; it was a life out of the pot, free to experience and be experienced within the ordinariness of being.

This is the challenge for the church, the nation and us as individuals. Do we wish to stay embedded in the transferred cultural myth of church and state or are we prepared to challenge that myth and develop relationships that are mature and robust, based on our acceptance of our past?

David Lose suggests, 'All we have to do is trade what we've been led to believe is life for the real thing.' [21]This is challenging. The hanging on to past myths, childhood hopes and dreams and another place and time gets in the way of us being at home in this place and time. It gets into the way of developing contextual myths, hopes and dreams applicable to now.

For the disciples, rattling the cages of tradition was safer than actually taking the costly steps to develop appropriate new

---

20   http://www.workingpreacher.org/craft.aspx?post=3542
21   http://www.workingpreacher.org/craft.aspx?post=1626

world views, to put into action the world view Jesus lived. Often people say they want to live like Jesus, to which I reply, 'What, you want to be grumpy, rude, difficult, alternative, disruptive, contrary and more?' Usually, they reply no, isn't he about love? Yes, he is about relationships and love but not in a warm and fuzzy way; it is confrontational and transformative.

The things we have been told and are embedded in our psyche are not necessarily life giving and freeing. We have to break that pot and engage at the real human level. Alan Brehm tells us, 'We only truly discover the life and love that God has to offer us when we let go all the things we cling to so tightly in that small place of "I" and open ourselves to the people around us in compassion, understanding, and love.'[22] It is this need to let go of the human things we cling tightly to that results in Jesus' savage rebuke of Peter. Are we deserving of such a rebuke?

In recent times, I have been challenged by actions of the Church and those within it in terms of its handling of the Child Abuse scandal, selling of churches, response to individuals within the LGBTI community, lack of inclusion for First Nations Peoples people and more. Similarly, I have been challenged by the actions of self confessing Christians at the leadership levels within our nation and their selective application of the idea of Freedom of Speech and Religion and to purport to speak on behalf of God on issues such as climate change, welfare and more. It is painful.

'I am talking about the pain of living on for Jesus in the midst of a dying church, a church too moribund to sail with the winds of change.' (Peter Woods, 2012)[23], particularly at the institutional level. It is also about individuals who are also unable to follow the Spirit into a new understanding of God in this place.

---

22 http://thewakingdreamer.blogspot.com/2012/03/hardest-choice-mk.html

23 https://thelisteninghermit.com/2012/09/11/is-your-martyrdom-also-discipleship-mark-827-38-ordinary-24b/

Yet, what I am interested in is how the Parish from where I write this, like many parishes across Australia, is taking Jesus seriously and letting go of preconceptions and the ways that have been normal here. Even before my time here, we had embraced diversity in gender and ability, we had supported ordination of women and the recognition of First Nations People sovereignty, supported refugees and developed an effective food collection for needy people. This has always been a parish that addressed issues and found itself changing how it worships and how it practised faith accordingly.

This parish is no longer just about what happens on Sunday, if it ever was, and has continued to find new ways to connect itself to the local community. As a result we are beginning to look different to the parish we once were. This is the point Jesus makes. Living in relationship to your context – in his case becoming human – forces you into a different shape and worldview.

His worldview changed remarkably over his life. If we take him seriously, ours will too.